Holy is the Lord

Exalt the Lord our God and Worship at His holy mountain for Holy is the Lord our God.

Psalm 99, vs. 9

BOOK OF LYRICS
*To be used with the audio cassettes
of Worship Music*
"Into Thy Presence"
"Lord, Draw Me Nearer"
"I Worship You"
"With All My Heart"
"Forever To Reign"
"In This Upper Room"

Jim Cowan

*Troubadour Music
Franciscan University Press
Franciscan University of Steubenville
Steubenville, Ohio 43952*

The HOLY IS THE LORD series was produced to assist individuals, prayer groups and parishes to develop worship in their prayer. The songs have been selected and arranged in such a way as to flow one into the next, to enhance worship by uplifting the mind and heart of the worshipper through songs.

The lyrics book is designed to be used with musical accompaniment provided either by the audio cassettes or by musicians.

The melody and chords book is designed for the musician. The songs, therefore, are in the order that lends itself to moving from one to the next easily.

Most of the songs in this collection are copyrighted. Further reproduction of any kind without the express permission of the copyright owner is in violation of the law. Please refer to the copyright acknowledgement underneath each song for the name and address of the respective copyright owner.

Cover design: Art Mancuso.
Copyright © 1988, 1989, 1991, 1992 Troubadour Music, Franciscan University Press, Franciscan University of Steubenville, Steubenville, Ohio 43952. All rights reserved.

Printed in the United States of America
ISBN 0-940535-38-6

CONTENTS

INTO THY PRESENCE

SIDE ONE
- Open Your Eyes 1
- My All in All 2
- As the Deer 3
- Make My Heart Your Dwelling Place 4
- Breathe on Me Holy One 5
- More Precious Than Silver 6
- I Exalt Thee 7
- Singing Hallelujah 8
- You Are Holy 9
- Glory to You 10

SIDE TWO
- Exodus XV 11
- I Will Call 12
- Into Thy Presence 13
- O Come, Let Us Worship 14
- Holy Is the Lord 15
- At the Name of Jesus 16
- Glory to the Lamb 17
- Lion of Judah 18
- We Bring the Sacrifice of Praise 19
- What a Mighty God 20
- He Has Made Me Glad 21
- He Is the King 22

LORD, DRAW ME NEARER

SIDE ONE
- Glory to the King 23
- I Will Magnify 24
- Glorify Thy Name 25
- Holy, Holy, Holy 26
- You Alone Are Holy 27
- Worthy Is the Lamb 28
- Change My Heart, O God 29
- Nearer Than Before 30
- Praise the Name of Jesus 31
- O Lord, God of Israel 32

SIDE TWO
- Mighty Is Our God 33
- Glory 34
- Hosanna 35
- Ascribe to the Lord 36
- Enter In 37
- Lord of All 38
- Worthy Is the Lamb (Who Was Slain) 39
- Thou Art Worthy 40
- Jesus the Lord 41
- Here I Am, Lord 42

I WORSHIP YOU

SIDE ONE
- Unto the House of the Lord 43
- Hallelujah, He Is Risen 44
- All Hail King Jesus 45
- Come Holy Ghost 46
- His Name Shall Be Called 47
- Holy God, We Praise Thy Name 48
- I Worship You 49
- Holy, Holy Lamb of God 50
- Give Thanks 51
- Jesus Has Done It All 52

SIDE TWO
- He Is Coming 53
- You Shall Be Clothed with Power 54
- Let the Fire Fall 55
- The Dwelling of God Is Among You Today 56
- Be Exalted, O God 57
- For You Are My God 58
- It Is Good 59
- Great and Wonderful 60
- We Belong to God 61
- You Are the Vine 62

WITH ALL MY HEART

SIDE ONE
- Glory, Glory To The King 63
- God Is My Refuge 64
- He That Is In Us 65
- Great And Mighty Army 66
- I Will Rejoice 67
- He Is Exalted 68
- Forever Grateful 69
- Salvation Belongs To Our God 70
- God Alone 71
- My God And My All 72
- Have Mercy On Me 73
- Holy Ground 74
- Standing On Holy Ground 75

SIDE TWO
- Raise Up An Army 76
- O Come Let Us Sing For Joy 77
- The Mighty One of Israel 78
- The God Of Israel Is Mighty 79
- Elohim, Adonai 80
- All Consuming Fire 81
- To Him Who Sits On The Throne 82
- We Are An Offering 83
- With All My Heart 84
- Sing Unto The Lord 85

FOREVER TO REIGN

SIDE ONE
- Surround Us Lord 86
- All Creation Worships You 87
- Forever To Reign 88
- Crown Him Lord Of Lords 89
- I Want To Know You 90
- Faithful To Your Call 91

SIDE TWO
- I Bow My Knee 92
- A Shield About Me 93
- Refiner's Fire 94
- Come Into My Heart 95
- I Will Pledge This Song To You 96
- We Exalt You 97

IN THIS UPPER ROOM

SIDE ONE
   In This Upper Room..........................98
   Spirit of God Medley 99
      A. Fire of God
      B. When The Spirit Sets Us Free
      C. Not By Might
      D. Jesus Reigns
   Let Us Rejoice And Be Glad 100
   I Long To See Your Face.....................101
   In Your Light 102
   I Dedicate My Heart 103

SIDE TWO
   Shine, Jesus, Shine..........................104
   Draw Me Nearer Medley 105
      A. More Of You
      B. That First Love
      C. Into Your Hands
      D. Immerse Me
      E. In Your Name
      F. I Love You Lord My King
      G. You Are My Hope O God
      H. God Of My Life, I Believe

OPEN YOUR EYES 1
By Carl Tuttle

Open your eyes see the glory of the King.
Lift up your voice and His praises sing.
I love You Lord, I will proclaim
Alleluia I bless Your name.

Copyright ©1985 Mercy Publishing, P.O. Box 65004, Anaheim, CA 92815, All rights reserved. International copyright secured. Used by permission.

MY ALL IN ALL 2
By Frank Hernandez and Sherry Saunders

You are my strength, O God.
You are my help, O God.
You are the One on whom I call.
You are my shield, O God.
My life I yield, O God.
For You will ever be my all in all.

Copyright ©1975 Sparrow Song Candle Company Music/Cherry River Music Company Sparrow Corporation, 9255 Deering Avenue, Chatsworth, CA 91311. All rights reserved. Used by permission.

AS THE DEER 3
By Martin Nystrom

As the deer panteth for the water,
So my soul longeth after Thee.
You alone are my heart's desire,
And I long to worship Thee.
You alone are my strength, my shield,
To You alone may my spirit yield.
You alone are my heart's desire,
And I long to worship Thee.

Copyright ©1984 Maranatha! Music, P.O. Box 1396, Costa Mesa, CA 92628. All rights reserved. Used by permission. International copyright secured.

4   MAKE MY HEART YOUR DWELLING PLACE
By Jim Cowan

Make my heart Your dwelling place,
A temple just for You;
A consecrated resting place,
A vessel ever true,
Make my heart a fire,
With the brightness of Your Son,
Make my heart a dwelling place,
For the Holy One.

Copyright ©1986 James A. Cowan, Steubenville Liturgical Resources, 745 Brady Avenue, Steubenville, OH 43952. All rights reserved. Used by permission.

5   BREATHE ON ME HOLY ONE
By Jim Cowan

Draw me to the Living waters,
Cleanse me in that crystal stream.
Wash me in the Waters of Life,
Seal me with the Spirit of Christ my Lord.
Breathe on me Breath of God,
Rest on me he'vnly Dove.
Breathe on me Holy One,
Come, Holy Spirit, come.

Copyright ©James A. Cowan, Steubenville Liturgical Resources, 745 Brady Avenue, Steubenville, OH 43952. All rights reserved. Used by permission.

6   MORE PRECIOUS THAN SILVER
By Lynn DeShazo

Lord You are more precious than silver.
Lord You are more costly than gold.
Lord You are more beautiful than diamonds
And nothing I desire compares with You.

Copyright ©1982 Integrity's Hosanna! Music, C/O Integrity Music P.O. Box 16813, Mobile, AL 36616. All rights reserved. International copyright secured. Used by permission.

I EXALT THEE 7
By Pete Sanchez

For Thou O Lord art high above all the earth.
Thou art exalted far above all Gods.
For Thou O Lord art high above all the earth.
Thou art exalted far above all Gods.
I exalt Thee, I exalt Thee.
I exalt Thee, Oh Lord.

Copyright ©1977 Pete Sanchez, 4723 Hickory Downs, Houston, TX 77084. Used by permission.

SINGING HALLELUJAH 8
By Jim Cowan

We have come to Mount Zion,
To the city of the Living God;
The heavenly Jerusalem,
With myriads of angels round the throne,
Singing Hallelujah, singing Hallelujah,
Singing Hallelujah.

And we've come unto Jesus,
Through the blood of the new covenant;
Made pure to stand before the throne of grace,
With all the first-born saints in endless praise!
Singing Hallelujah, singing Hallelujah,
Singing Hallelujah.

Since we've found such a kingdom
Which shall never be removed,
Let us worship the Lord in fear and awe,
In reverence and heartfelt gratitude!
Singing Hallelujah, singing Hallelujah,
Singing Hallelujah.

Copyright ©1985 James A. Cowan, Steubenville Liturgical Resources, 745 Brady Avenue, Steubenville, OH 43952. All rights reserved. Used by permission.

9   YOU ARE HOLY
By Donald Fishel

Holy, You are holy.
Holy, Almighty Lord,
Who was, Who is and is to come.
You are holy, You are holy.

Worthy, You are worthy.
Worthy, Almighty Lord,
For You have created everything.
You are worthy, You are worthy Lord.

Copyright ©1979 The Word of God, P.O. Box 8617, Ann Arbor, MI 48107 U.S.A., All rights reserved. Used by permission.

10   GLORY TO YOU
By Jim Cowan

Oh Lion of Judah, the Lamb that was slain,
The Hope of the nations, Messiah and King,
The Source of Salvation, Faithful and True,
Oh Blessed Redeemer we worship You.

Glory to You, King Jesus, Glory and praise!
Glory to You, Lord Jesus, Glory and praise to You!

Copyright ©1986 James A. Cowan, Steubenville Liturgical Resources, 745 Brady Avenue, Steubenville, OH 43952. All rights reserved. Used by permission.

EXODUS XV
By Frank Gallio

The Lord is my strength and my song.
And He is become my salvation,
He is my God.

REFRAIN
And I shall prepare Him my heart,
And I shall prepare Him my heart,
And I shall prepare Him my heart.

The Lord, He shall reign
Forever and ever, Amen.
The Lord, He shall reign
Forever and ever, Amen.

REFRAIN

Copyright © 1982 Mercy Publishing, P.O. Box 65004, Anaheim, CA 92815. All rights reserved. International copyright secured. Used by permission.

I WILL CALL
By Victor Rubbo

I will call,
Upon the Lord,
Who is worthy
To be praised.
I will call,
Upon the Lord,
Who is worthy,
To be praised.
So shall I be saved,
So shall I be saved,
From my enemies.

Copyright ©1982 Mercy Publishing, P.O. Box 65004, Anaheim, CA 92815. All rights reserved. International copyright secured. Used with permission.

13 INTO THY PRESENCE
By Jim Cowan

Draw us nearer into Thy presence Lord,
That we might in one accord give praise to the Lamb of God.
Draw us deeper unto the throne of grace
That we might behold Thy face and worship the Lamb.
You are the Holy one, Lord Jesus
You are the Lamb of God.
You've shed Your precious blood,
Through the vale we enter now
Into Thy holy place,
With our offering of praise,
You are my Hope, You are my Rock,
Your faithfulness enduring forever.
You are my all. You are my Savior.
Your mercy is so bountiful
I offer you a sacrifice of praise.

Copyright ©1988 James A. Cowan, Steubenville Liturgical Resources, 745 Brady Avenue, Steubenville, OH 43952. All rights reserved. Used by permission.

14 O COME LET US WORSHIP
By Jim Cowan

O come let us worship and bow down,
Let us kneel before the Lord our Maker,
For He is our Father, our Rock, our Redeemer,
And we are the flock of His hand.

If today you hear My voice,
Harden not your hearts.
But open wide the door to Me,
And I shall give you life.

Copyright ©1985 James A. Cowan, Steubenville Liturgical Resources, 745 Brady Avenue, Steubenville, OH 43952. All rights reserved. Used by permission.

HOLY IS THE LORD 15
By Brain Beshears

Holy (Echo), is the Lord (Echo),
Holy (Echo), is the Lord (Echo),
Holy, Holy, Holy is the Lord.

Worthy (Echo), is the Lord (Echo),
Worthy (Echo), is the Lord (Echo),
Worthy, Worthy, Worthy is the Lord.

Jesus (Echo), is the Lord (Echo),
Jesus (Echo), is the Lord (Echo),
Jesus, Jesus, Jesus is the Lord.

Holy (Echo), is the Lord (Echo),
Holy (Echo), is the Lord (Echo),
Holy, Holy, Holy is the Lord.

Copyright ©1981 Brian L. Beshears, Administered by Mercy Publishing, P.O. Box 65004, Anaheim, CA 92815. All rights reserved. International copyright secured. Used by permission.

16 AT THE NAME OF JESUS
By Jim Cowan

At the name of Jesus ev'ry knee shall bow;
Ev'ry tongue confess Him, King of Glory now.
Tis the Father's pleasure we should call Him Lord,
Who from the beginning was the mighty Word.

Humbled for a season to receive a name;
From the lips of sinners unto which He came.
Faithfully He bore it, spotless to the last,
Brought it back victorious when through death He passed.

Bore it up triumphant with its human light,
Through all ranks of creatures to the central height.
To the throne of Godhead, to the Father's breast,
Filled it with the glory of that perfect rest.

In your hearts enthrone Him, there let Him subdue,
All that is not holy, all that is not true.
Crown Him as your Captain in temptation's hour;
Let His will enfold you in it's light and power.

Jesus Lord and Savior shall return again,
With His Father's Glory o'er the earth to reign.
For all wreaths of Empire meet upon His brow,
And our hearts confess Him, King of Glory now.

Copyright ©1986 James A. Cowan, Steubenville Liturgical Resources, 745 Brady Avenue, Steubenville, OH 43952. All rights reserved. Used by permission.

17 GLORY TO THE LAMB
By Larry Dempsey

Glory, glory, glory to the Lamb.
Glory, glory, glory to the Lamb.
For He is glorious and worthy to be praised,
The Lamb upon the throne;
And unto Him we lift our voice in praise,
The Lamb upon the throne.

Copyright ©1983 ZionSong Music, ASCAP P.O. Box 101050, Palm Bay, FL 32910. All rights reserved. International copyright secured. Used by permission.

LION OF JUDAH

By Ted Sandquist

Lion of Judah, on the throne,
I shout Your name, let it be known
That You are King of Kings,
You are the Prince of Peace.
May Your Kingdom's reign never cease!
Hail to the King!
Hail to the King!

Lion of Judah, come to earth,
I want to thank You for Your birth.
For the living Word,
For Your death on the tree,
For Your resurrection victory!
Hallelujah! Hallelujah!

Lion of Judah, come again,
Take up Your throne, Jerusalem.
Bring release to this earth,
And the consummation
Of Your Kingdom's reign, let it come!
Maranatha! Maranatha!

Lion of Judah, on the throne,
I shout Your name. Let it be known
That You are King of Kings,
You are the Prince of Peace.
May Your Kingdom's reign never cease!
Hail to the King!
Hail to the King!
Hail to the King!
Hail to the King!
You are my King!

Copyright ©1976 Lion of Judah Music, 365 Great Circle Road, Nashville, TN 37228. All rights reserved. Reprinted by permission of the Benson Company.

19 WE BRING THE SACRIFICE OF PRAISE
By Kirk Dearman

We bring the sacrifice of praise into the house of the Lord;
We bring the sacrifice of praise into the house of the Lord.
And we offer up to You the sacrifices of thanksgiving;
And we offer up to You the sacrifices of joy.

Copyright ©1984 Stamps-Baxter Administered by Zondervan, 365 Great Circle Road, Nashville, TN 37228. All rights reserved. Used by permission.

20 WHAT A MIGHTY GOD
Author Unknown

What a mighty God we serve.
What a mighty God we serve.
Angels bow before Him,
Heav'n and earth adore Him,
What a mighty God we serve.

21 HE HAS MADE ME GLAD
By Leona Von Brethorst

I will enter His gates with thanksgiving in my heart.
I will enter His courts with praise.
I will say this is the day that the Lord has made,
I will rejoice for He has made me glad.
He has made me glad.
He has made me glad.
I will rejoice for He has made me glad.
He has made me glad, He has made me glad.
I will rejoice for He has made me glad.

Copyright ©1976 Maranatha! Music, P.O. Box 1396, Costa Mesa, CA 92628. All rights reserved. Used by permission.

HE IS THE KING 22
Author Unknown

He is the King (Echo) of Kings (Echo).
He is the Lord (Echo) of Lords (Echo).
His name is Jesus (Echo), Jesus (Echo), Jesus (Echo), Jesus (Echo).
Oh - He is the King.

GLORY TO THE KING 23
By Tom McLain

Glory, Glory, Glory to the King!
Glory, Glory, Glory to the King!
Who is the King of glory?
King Jesus is His Name!
He is high and lifted up above the earth
And His Name I will proclaim!

Copyright ©1984 Glory Alleluia Music. All Rights exclusively controlled by Tempo Music Publications, Inc. Used with special permission.

I WILL MAGNIFY 24
By Scott Palazzo

I will magnify Thy name above all the earth;
I will magnify Thy name above all the earth;

I will sing unto Thee
The praises in my heart;
I will sing unto Thee
The praises in my heart.

I will sing unto Thee
The praises in my heart;
I will sing unto Thee
The praises in my heart.

Copyright ©1985 Mercy Publishing, P.O. Box 65004, Anaheim, CA 92815. All rights reserved. International copyright secured. Used by permission.

25 GLORIFY THY NAME
By Donna Adkins

Father, we love Thee, we praise Thee, we adore Thee.
Glorify Thy name in all the earth.
Glorify Thy name.
Glorify Thy name.
Glorify Thy name in all the earth.

Jesus, we love Thee, we praise Thee, we adore Thee.
Glorify Thy name in all the earth.
Glorify Thy name.
Glorify Thy name.
Glorify Thy name in all the earth.

Spirit, we love Thee, we praise Thee, we adore Thee.
Glorify Thy name in all the earth.
Glorify Thy name.
Glorify Thy name
Glorify Thy name in all the earth.

Copyright ©1976, 1981 Maranatha! Music, P.O. Box 1396, Costa Mesa, CA 92628. All rights reserved. International copyright secured. Used by permission.

26 HOLY, HOLY, HOLY
Public Domain

Holy, Holy, Holy! Lord God Almighty!
Early in the morning our song shall rise to Thee;
Holy, Holy, Holy! merciful and mighty,
God in three Persons, blessed Trinity.

Holy, Holy, Holy! all the Saints adore Thee,
Casting down their golden crowns around the glassy sea;
Cherubim and seraphim falling down before Thee,
Which wert, and art, and ever more shalt be.

Holy, Holy, Holy! though the darkness hide Thee,
Though the eye of sinful man Thy glory may not see,
Only Thou art holy; there is none beside Thee,
Perfect in pow'r, in love and purity.

Holy, Holy, Holy! Lord God Almighty!
All thy works shall praise Thy Name in earth, and sky and sea;
Holy, Holy, Holy! merciful and mighty,
God in three Persons, blessed Trinity.

YOU ALONE ARE HOLY

By Jim Cowan

REFRAIN
O Lord God Almighty, O Lord most holy,
You are King of Kings, and Lord of Lords,
The Father of us all;
And we bow down before You,
Ev'ry creature shall adore You,
You are Mighty God, the Messiah,
The Savior of the world.

You alone are holy, You alone O Lord
You alone are worthy, Lamb of God.

REFRAIN

We behold Your splendor,
Seated on the throne,
Robed and crowned with glory,
Ever more.

We behold Your splendor,
Seated on the throne,
Robed and crowned with glory,
Ever more.
Mighty Lord!

Copyright ©1985 James A. Cowan, Steubenville Liturgical Resources, 745 Brady Avenue, Steubenville, OH 43952. All rights reserved. Used by permission.

28 WORTHY IS THE LAMB
Author Unknown

Worthy is the Lamb.
Worthy is the Lamb.
Worthy is the Lamb.
Worthy is the Lamb.

Jesus is the Lamb.
Jesus is the Lamb.
Jesus is the Lamb.
Jesus is the Lamb.

Glory to the Lamb.
Glory to the Lamb.
Glory to the Lamb.
Glory to the Lamb.

Worthy is the Lamb.
Worthy is the Lamb.
Worthy is the Lamb.
Worthy is the Lamb.

29 CHANGE MY HEART, O GOD
By Eddie Espinosa

Change my heart Oh God,
Make it ever true.
Change my heart Oh God,
May I be like You.

You are the potter,
I am the clay,
Mold me and make me,
This is what I pray.

Copyright ©1982 Mercy Publishing, P.O. 65004, Anaheim, CA 92815. All rights reserved. International copyright secured. Used by permission.

NEARER THAN BEFORE 30
By Jim Cowan

Lord take the blindness from my eyes,
All my arrogance and pride,
Fill my vision with Your light.
And Lord take the deafness from my ears,
When I'm dull and slow to hear,
Help me recognize Your voice.

REFRAIN
Lord draw me nearer than before,
Every day I long for more of You to know and see Your face.
Lord draw me deeper into prayer.
Every day I want to meet You there,
Just to spend my life with You.

Lord take the darkness from my mind.
When confusion makes me blind,
Come renew me with Your truth.
And Lord take the hardness from my heart,
Roll away the stony part,
Fill me with a love that's true.

REFRAIN

Copyright ©1988 James A. Cowan, Steubenville Liturgical Resources, 745 Brady Avenue, Steubenville, OH 43952. All rights reserved. Used by permission.

PRAISE THE NAME OF JESUS 31
By Roy Hicks, Jr.

Praise the name of Jesus.
Praise the name of Jesus.
He's my rock, He's my fortress,
He's my deliverer, In Him will I trust.
Praise the name of Jesus.

Praise the name of Jesus.
Praise the name of Jesus.
He's my rock, He's my fortress,
He's my deliverer,
In Him will I trust,
Praise the name of Jesus.

Copyright ©1976 Latter Rain Music. All rights reserved. Used by permission of Sparrow Corporation, 9255 Deering Avenue, Chatsworth, CA 91311.

32   O LORD GOD OF ISRAEL
By Donna Adkins

O Lord God of Israel,
There is no God like Thee in the heav'n,
There is no God like Thee in the earth,
O Lord God of Israel
That keepeth covenant and showeth mercy,
Unto Thy servants that walk before Thee,
With all of their hearts.

Copyright ©1976 Integrity's Hosanna! Music, C/O Integrity Music, Inc., P.O. Box 16813, Mobile, AL 36616. All rights reserved. Used by permission.

33   MIGHTY IS OUR GOD
By Steve Alaniz

REFRAIN
Hallelujah, hallelujah, hallelujah, hallelujah!
Hallelujah, hallelujah, hallelujah, hallelujah!

Mighty is our God, the everlasting King.
All the earth proclaim the glories of His name.
Enthroned in the heavens, the angels sing His praise.
Mighty is our God! Holy is He!

REFRAIN

Praise Him, sun and moon. Praise Him, stars of light.
Praise Him in the depths, and praise Him in the heights.
Let the heavens be glad and the earth rejoice.
Mighty is our God! Holy is He!

REFRAIN

Witness to all men the joy of the Lord.
For upon us all His love He has poured.
Let every tongue confess forever:
Jesus is Lord! Worthy is He!

REFRAIN

Copyright ©1976 Steve Alaniz, Catholic Services of Dallas, Texas Inc., 4530 San Gabriel Drive, Dallas, TX 75229. All rights reserved. Used by permission.

GLORY   34
By Danny Daniels

Glory, glory in the highest,
Glory, to the Almighty;
Glory to the Lamb of God.
And glory to the living Word;
Glory to the Lamb!

I give glory. (Echo) Glory.
Glory. (Echo) Glory.
Glory, glory to the Lamb.
Glory, glory to the Lamb.

Glory, glory in the highest,
Glory, to the Almighty;
Glory to the Lamb of God.
And glory to the living Word;
Glory to the Lamb!

I give glory. (Echo) Glory.
Glory. (Echo) Glory.
Glory, glory to the Lamb.
I give glory to the Lamb. (Last time, sing 3 times)

Copyright ©1987 Mercy Publishing, P.O. Box 65004, Anaheim, CA 92815. All rights reserved. International copyright secured. Used by permission.

HOSANNA   35
By Carl Tuttle

Hosanna, Hosanna, Hosanna in the highest.
Hosanna, Hosanna, Hosanna in the highest.
Lord, we lift up Your Name,
With hearts full of praise.
Be exalted, O Lord my God.
Hosanna in the highest.

Glory, Glory, Glory to the King of Kings,
Glory, Glory, Glory to the King of Kings,
Lord, we lift up Your Name,
With hearts full of praise.
Be exalted, O Lord my God
Glory to the King of Kings.

Copyright ©1985 Mercy Publishing, P.O. Box 65004, Anaheim, CA 92815. All rights reserved. International copyright reserved. Used by permission.

36   ASCRIBE TO THE LORD
By James Berlucchi

(Women)
Ascribe to the Lord, O heavenly beings,
Ascribe to Him glory and strength.
O come ascribe to the Lord the glory of His name,
And worship Him in holy array.

(Men)
The voice of God is upon many waters.
The God of glory thundering forth.
The voice of God, full of majesty and power.

REFRAIN
(Women)
Hallelujah! Hallelujah! Hallelujah! Hallelujah!
(Men)
The voice of the Lord breaks the cedars of Lebanon.
The voice of the Lord flashes forth flames of fire.
The voice of the Lord strips the oaks and forests bare.
And in His temple all cry, 'Glory!'

(Women)
The Lord sits enthroned over all the flood.
From there He reigns, enthroned as King forever,
Giving His strength to the people who know His name.
The Lord blessing His people with peace.

(Men)
The voice of God is upon many waters.
The God of glory thundering forth.
The voice of God full of majesty and power.

REFRAIN

Copyright ©1981 Word of God, P.O. Box 8617, Ann Arbor, MI 48107. All rights reserved.

ENTER IN 37
By George Misulia

Enter in, enter in, I am free to enter in.
In His name, in His blood, in His Spirit I come freely
To the throne of grace and worship face to face.
O praise the living God!
I am free, I am free to enter in. (Repeat verse)

Copyright ©1985 Crossroads, 207 North Rock Glen Road, Apt. I, Baltimore, MD 21229. All rights reserved. Used by permission.

LORD OF ALL 38
By Jim Cowan

Jesus You are my hope.
Jesus You are my Life.
Hope of the homeless.
Light of the World.
Sinners refuge, Emmanuel.

Jesus You are my hope.
Jesus You are my Life.
Hope of the homeless.
Light of the World.
Sinners refuge, Emmanuel.

Lord of all. Lord of all.
Hope of the homeless.
Light of the World.
Sinners refuge, Emmanuel.
Lord of all. Lord of all. Lord of all.

Copyright ©1988 James A. Cowan, Steubenville Liturgical Resources, 745 Brady Avenue, Steubenville, OH 43952. All rights reserved. Used by permission.

39   **WORTHY IS THE LAMB**
                        (WHO WAS SLAIN)
                            By Roger Holtz

Worthy is the Lamb who was slain,
To receive power and wealth,
And wisdom and might.
Honor, Glory, Blessing, Power.
Worthy is the Lamb who was slain.

Copyright ©1982 Roger Holtz, 3225 Edgewood Drive, Ann Arbor, MI 48104. All rights reserved. Used by permission.

40   **THOU ART WORTHY**
                        By Pauline M. Mills
                       (Based on Rev. 4:11, 5:9)

Thou art worthy. Thou art worthy.
Thou art worthy, O Lord.
Thou art worthy to receive glory,
Glory and honor and power.
For Thou hast created, hast all things created,
For Thou hast created all things,
And for Thy pleasure they are created.
Thou art worthy O Lord.

Copyright ©1963, 1975 Fred Bock Music Company, P.O. Box 333, Tarzana, CA 91356 All rights reserved. Used by permission.

JESUS THE LORD

By Roc O'Connor, S.J.

REFRAIN
Jesus. Jesus. Let all creation bend the knee to the Lord.

In Him we live, we move and have our being;
In Him the Christ, in Him the King!
Jesus, the Lord.

REFRAIN

Though Son, He did not cling to godliness;
But emptied Himself, became a slave!
Jesus, the Lord.

REFRAIN

He lived obediently His Father's will,
Accepting His death, death on a tree!
Jesus, the Lord.

REFRAIN

Copyright ©1981 North American Liturgical Resources, 10802 North 23rd Avenue, Phoenix, AZ 85029 All rights reserved. Used by permission.

42   HERE I AM, LORD
By Dan Shutte, S.J.

I, the Lord of sea and sky.
I have heard My people cry.
All who dwell in dark and sin,
My hand will save.
I who made the stars of night,
I will make their darkness bright.
Who will bear My light to them?
Whom shall I send?

REFRAIN
Here I am, Lord. Is it I, Lord?
I have heard You calling in the night.
I will go, Lord, if You lead me.
I will hold Your people in my heart.

I, the Lord of snow and rain,
I have borne My people's pain.
I have wept for love of them.
They turn away.
I will break their hearts of stone,
Give them hearts for love alone.
I will speak My word to them.
Whom shall I send?

REFRAIN

I, the Lord of wind and flame,
I will tend the poor and lame.
I will set a feast for them.
My hand will save.
Finest bread I will provide,
Till their hearts be satisfied.
I will give My life to them.
Whom shall I send?

REFRAIN

Copyright ©1981 North American Liturgical Resources, 10802 North 23rd Avenue, Phoenix, AZ 85029. All rights reserved. Used by permission.

UNTO THE HOUSE OF THE LORD

By John Bagniewski

REFRAIN
I rejoiced when they said to me,
"Let us go unto the house of the Lord,"
Standing there O Jerusalem,
In your gates unto the house of the Lord.

Look upon Jerusalem, the city now restored.
Here the tribes of Yahweh come as one unto the Lord.

REFRAIN

As He ordered Israel, they come to praise His name,
Here where courts of justice, the courts of David reign.

REFRAIN

Pray for peace, Jerusalem, prosperity at home,
Peace inside your city walls that comes from God alone.

REFRAIN

Since we are God's people, I say, "Peace be to you!"
May the God who dwells in us your happiness renew.

REFRAIN

Copyright ©1978, Servants of the Lord, assigned to People of Praise, Inc., 705 SE 12th Avenue, Minneapolis, MN 55414. All rights reserved. Used by permission.

44   HALLELUJAH, HE IS RISEN!

By Jim Cowan and John Flaherty

Hallelujah, Hallelujah, Hallelujah, He is risen!
Hallelujah, Hallelujah, Hallelujah, He is risen!

Behold the stone that's rolled away,
Behold the shroud and the empty grave.
Behold the Lamb who paid this price
Behold your Savior, Jesus Christ!

Hallelujah, Hallelujah, Hallelujah, He is risen!
Hallelujah, Hallelujah, Hallelujah, He is risen!

The power of death could not contain the Lamb,
The chains of sin and death could not bind Him down;
O death where is your sting now the tomb is empty,
O death where is your victory, now that Jesus lives!

Hallelujah, Hallelujah, Hallelujah, He is risen!
Hallelujah, Hallelujah, Hallelujah, He is risen!

Behold His feet once crucified
Touch His hands and wounded side.
Behold the Lamb who bled and died
Behold your Savior now glorified!

Hallelujah, Hallelujah, Hallelujah, He is risen!
Hallelujah, Hallelujah, Hallelujah, He is risen!

The Lord is here robed as a warrior
Clothed in power and strength
His might and truth unfurled
Reach out your hand and touch the mighty healer
For He is our deliverer the Savior of the World.

Hallelujah, Hallelujah, Hallelujah, He is risen!
Hallelujah, Hallelujah, Hallelujah, He is risen.
He is risen from the dead!

Copyright ©1985 James A. Cowan and John Flaherty, Steubenville Liturgical Resources, 745 Brady Avenue, Steubenville, OH 43952. All rights reserved. Used by permission.

ALL HAIL KING JESUS 45
By Dave Moody

All Hail King Jesus, All Hail Emmanuel,
King of Kings, Lord of Lords, bright morning star
And for all eternity I'll ever praise you
And forevermore I will reign with you.

Copyright ©1981 Glory Alleluia Music, All rights exclusively controlled by Tempo Music Publication, Inc., 2712 West 104 Terrace, Leawood, KS 66206. Used with special permission.

COME HOLY GHOST 46
Public Domain

Come Holy Ghost, Creator blest,
And in our hearts take up Thy rest.
Come with Thy grace and heav'nly aid
To fill the hearts which Thou hast made.
To fill the hearts which Thou hast made.

O Comforter, to Thee we cry.
Thou heavn'ly gift of God most high.
Thou font of life and fire of love.
And sweet anointing from above,
And sweet anointing from above.

Praise be to Thee, Father and Son.
And Holy Spirit, three in one.
And may the Son on us bestow,
The gifts that from the Spirit flow.
The gifts that from the Spirit flow.

HIS NAME SHALL BE CALLED 47
Music: Public Domain
Words: Author Unknown

His name, His name shall be called Wonderful
His name, His name shall be called Counselor
The Mighty God, the Everlasting Father.
The Prince of Peace for all eternity.
The Mighty God, the Everlasting Father.
The Prince of Peace for all eternity.

48 HOLY GOD, WE PRAISE THY NAME
Copyright Unknown

Holy God, we praise Thy Name!
Lord of all we bow before Thee;
All on earth Thy sceptre claim,
All in heav'n above adore Thee;
Infinite Thy vast domain,
Everlasting is Thy reign.
Infinite Thy vast domain,
Everlasting is Thy reign.

Hark! the loud celestial hymn
Angel choirs above are raising;
Cherubim and Seraphim,
In unceasing chorus praising;
Fill the heav'ns with sweet accord;
Holy, Holy, Holy Lord!
Fill the heav'ns with sweet accord;
Holy, Holy, Holy Lord!

I WORSHIP YOU 49
By Carl Tuttle

I give you all the honor and praise that's due Your Name,
For You are the King of Glory, the Creator of all things.

REFRAIN
And I worship You, I give my life to You,
I fall down on my knees,
Yes, I worship You, I give my life to You,
I fall down on my knees.

As Your Spirit moves upon me now, You meet my deepest need,
And I lift my hands up to Your throne, Your mercy, I've received.

REFRAIN

You have broken chains that bound me, You've set this captive free,
I will lift my voice to praise Your Name for all eternity.

And I worship You, I give my life to You.
I fall down on my knees,
Yes, I worship You, I give my life to You,
I fall down on my knees.
I worship you.

Copyright ©1982 Mercy Publishing, P.O. Box 65004, Anaheim, CA 92815. All right reserved. International copyright secured. Used by permission.

HOLY HOLY LAMB OF GOD 50
By Jim Cowan

Let us enter through the open door into the heart of God.
Let us drink of living waters flowing from His throne.
Let us give ourselves completely in the presence of our God.
Let us bow in adoration, and worship Him.
Holy, Holy, Holy Lord, Holy, Holy Lamb of God.
Holy, Holy, Holy Lord, Holy, Holy Lamb of God.

Copyright ©1988, James A. Cowan, Steubenville Liturgical Resources, 745 Brady Avenue, Steubenville, OH 43952. All rights reserved. Used by permission.

51 GIVE THANKS
By Henry Smith

Give thanks with a grateful heart.
Give thanks to the Holy One.
Give thanks because He's given Jesus Christ, His Son.

And now let the weak say "I am strong;"
Let the poor say "I am rich"
Because of what the Lord has done for us.
And now let the weak say "I am strong;"
Let the poor say "I am rich"
Because of what the Lord has done for us.
Give thanks.

Copyright ©1978 Integrity's Hosanna! Music, C/O Integrity Music, Inc., P.O. Box 16813, Mobile, AL 36616. All rights reserved. Used by permission.

52 JESUS HAS DONE IT ALL
By Jim and Mary Cowan

Jesus has done it all.
He is our victory,
Our life, our hope, our only joy.
Jesus had done it all.

Copyright ©1987 James A. and Mary Cowan, Steubenville Liturgical Resources, 745 Brady Avenue, Steubenville, OH 43952. All rights reserved. Used by permission.

53 HE IS COMING
By Jim Cowan

The Day of the Lord is at hand,
See Him riding on a white horse.
The armies of heaven behind Him,
And the Sword of the Spirit in His hand;
He will smite His enemies!
Halleluia! Halleluia! Halleluia,
He is coming!

His face is as bright as the sun,
His eyes are blazing like fire,
And His sword is shining like silver,
And He has victory written on His heart.
He will smite His enemies!
Halleluia! Halleluia! Halleluia,
He is coming!

Copyright ©1986 James A. Cowan, Steubenville Liturgical Resources, 745 Brady Avenue, Steubenville, OH 43952. All rights reserved. Used by permission.

YOU SHALL BE CLOTHED WITH POWER 54
By Jim Cowan

REFRAIN
You shall be clothed with power from on high,
When the Holy Spirit comes to you,
And you shall be My witnesses
Throughout the ends of the earth.
Throughout the ends of the earth.

Go forth to all the World,
And tell the good news,
Proclaim God's Kingdom has come
Through the triumph of His Son!

REFRAIN

The works that I have done
You also shall do
And still there's more to come
For My Spirit rests on you!

REFRAIN

The deaf shall hear My voice
The blind shall see.
The lame shall leap for joy,
And the captives shall be free.

Copyright ©1988 James A. Cowan, Steubenville Liturgical Resources, 745 Brady Avenue, Steubenville, OH 43952. All rights reserved. Used by permission.

55 LET THE FIRE FALL
By George Misulia

Holy Spirit, (Echo) come with Your fire!
Holy Spirit, (Echo) come with Your fire!
Holy Spirit, come with Your fire!
Holy Spirit, come with Your fire!

REFRAIN
Come Holy Spirit. Let the fire fall!
Come Holy Spirit. Let the fire fall!
Let the fire fall!
Let the fire fall!

Holy Spirit, (Echo) purify my heart!
Holy Spirit, (Echo) purify my heart!
Holy Spirit, purify my heart!
Holy Spirit, purify my heart!

REFRAIN

Holy Spirit, (Echo) set my life on fire!
Holy Spirit, (Echo) set my life on fire!
Holy Spirit, set my life on fire!
Holy Spirit, set me life on fire!

Copyright ©1984 Crossroads, 207 North Rock Glen Road, Apt. I, Baltimore, MD 21229. All rights reserved. Used by permission.

56 THE DWELLING OF GOD IS AMONG YOU TODAY
By Don Austin
(Based on Rev. 21)

And then I heard a loud voice say,
Behold, the dwelling of God is among you today!
And He shall wipe away your tears;
There'll be no mourning, or crying, or pain or death any more!
Hallelujah! Hallelujah!
For the Lord God Almighty,
Omnipotent reigns!
Our mighty God! Our risen Lord!
All the glory, and honor, and power are Yours ever more!

Copyright ©1979 Don Austin, 4248 Commonwealth, Detroit, MI 48208. Used by permission.

BE EXALTED, O GOD

By Brent Chambers

I will give thanks to Thee, O Lord, among the people.
I will sing praises to Thee among the nations.
For Thy steadfast love is great,
Is great to the heavens,
And Thy faithfulness, Thy faithfulness to the clouds.

Be exalted, O God,
Above the heavens.
Let Thy glory be over all the earth.
Be exalted, O God,
Above the heavens.
Let Thy glory be over all the earth.

I will give thanks to Thee, O Lord, among the people.
I will sing praises to Thee among the nations.
For Thy steadfast love is great,
Is great to the heavens,
And Thy faithfulness, Thy faithfulness to the clouds.

Be exalted, O God,
Above the heavens.
Let Thy glory be over all the earth.
Be exalted, O God,
Above the heavens.
Let Thy glory,
Let Thy glory,
Let Thy glory be over all the earth.

Copyright ©1977 Scripture in Song, Ltd., Administered by Maranatha Music, P.O. Box 1396, Costa Mesa, CA 92628. All rights reserved. Used by permission.

58   FOR YOU ARE MY GOD

By John Foley, S.J.

REFRAIN
For You are my God.
You alone are my joy;
Defend me, O Lord.

You give marvelous comrades to me;
The faithful who dwell in Your land;
Those who choose alien gods
Have chosen an alien band.

REFRAIN

You are my portion and cup;
It is You that I claim for my prize.
Your heritage is my delight;
The lot You have given to me.

REFRAIN

Glad are my heart and my soul;
Securely my body shall rest.
For You will not leave me for dead;
Nor lead Your beloved astray.

REFRAIN

You show me the path for my life;
In Your presence the fullness of joy.
To be at Your right hand forever
For me would be happiness always.

REFRAIN

Copyright ©1970 American Liturgy Resources, 10802. North 23rd Avenue, Phoenix, AZ 85029. All rights reserved. Used by permission.

IT IS GOOD 59
By Paul Wilbur

It is good to praise the Lord,
And make music to Your name, O God Most High,
To proclaim Your love and faithfulness
All the day and through the night.

REFRAIN
Lai-la-lai, lai-la-lai-la-lai,
la-la-lai-lai, lai-la-lai-la-lai-la-lai,
La-la-la-la-la-la-lai-la-lai,
La-la-lai-lai-lai-lai-lai!

You make me glad by Your deeds, O Lord,
So I sing for joy at all Your hands have made.
How great are Your works, O Lord
Elohim baruch hashem!

REFRAIN

May I dwell in Your courts, O Lord,
There to flourish like the trees of Lebanon
Planted in the house of Adonai there to live forevermore!

Copyright ©1985 Israel's Hope, 9057B Gaither Road, Gaithersburg, MD 20877. All rights reserved. Used by permission.

GREAT AND WONDERFUL 60
By Stuart Dauermann

Great and wonderful are Thy wonderous deeds,
O Lord God, the Almighty.
Just and true are all Thy ways, O Lord;
King of the ages art Thou.
Who shall not fear and glorify Thy name, O Lord?
For Thou alone art holy Thou alone.
All the nations shall come and worship Thee,
For Thy glory shall be revealed.
Hallelujah! Hallelujah! Hallelujah! Amen.
La la la la la__la la la la la la
La la la la la__la la la la la la
La la la la la__la la la la la la
La la la la la__la la la la la la!

Copyright ©1972 Lillenas Publishing Company, Box 419527, Kansas City, MO 64141. All rights reserved. Used by permission.

61   WE BELONG TO GOD
By John Flaherty

None of us lives as his own
And none of us dies as his own
For while we live we are responsible to God
And when we die, we die, as His servants.

REFRAIN
For both in life and death we belong to God,
That is why Christ has died for us and come again.
We shall all appear before the judgement seat of God
For it is written,
"Ev'ry knee shall bend before Me
And ev'ry tongue shall give praise to God."

For we are sure that neither death nor life,
Nor this nor future ages nor their pow'rs,
No height, no depth, no creature that thrives,
Will come between us and the love of Christ.

REFRAIN

Give yourselves as sacrifice to God,
Holy and acceptable to the Lord.
Do not allow your minds to be conformed to this age,
But let your hearts be ruled by His Spirit.

REFRAIN

Now not all of us shall fall asleep,
But all of us are to be changed;
In the twinkling of an eye,
As the last trumpet sounds,
We shall rise victorious in Christ!

Copyright ©1985 John Flaherty, Steubenville Liturgical Resources,
745 Brady Avenue, Steubenville, OH 43952. All rights reserved.
International copyright secured. Used by permission.

YOU ARE THE VINE

By Danny Daniels

You are the vine,
We are the branches;
Keep us abiding in You.
You are the vine,
We are the branches;
Keep us abiding in You.
And we'll go in Your love;
And we'll go in Your name;
That the world will surely know
That You have power to heal and to save.
You are the vine
We are the branches;
Keep us abiding in You.

Copyright ©1985 Mercy Publishing, P.O. Box 65004, Anaheim, CA 92815. All rights reserved. Used by permission.

63 GLORY, GLORY TO THE KING
By Phil White

REFRAIN
Glory, glory to the King of kings.
Glory, glory to the Lamb.
Glory, glory to the King of kings.
Glory, glory to the Lamb.
(Repeat)

God our righteousness
Enthroned,
High above the earth,
Has redeemed us
From the curse of sin.
That we might reign
With Him on high.

REFRAIN

He has clothed us
With salvation,
Wrapped us in
His righteousness.
To proclaim to ev'ry nation,
The glories of
His majesty on high.

REFRAIN

Glory to the Lamb.

©1988 Integrity's Hosanna Music, P.O. Box 16801, Mobile, AL 36616. Used by permission

GOD IS MY REFUGE 64
By Judy Horner Montemayor

God is my refuge and God is my strength,
A very present help in trouble.
God is my refuge and God is my strength,
A very present help in trouble.

Therefore I, will not fear,
Though the earth be removed,
And though the mountains,
Be carried into the midst of the sea.

©1973 Integrity's Hosanna Music, P.O. Box 16801, Mobile, AL 36616. Used by permission.

HE THAT IS IN US 65
By Graham Kendrick

He that is in us is greater than he
That is in the world.
He that is in us is greater than he
That is in the world.

©1986 Thankyou Music, Maranatha Music, P.O. Box 1396, Costa Mea, CA 92628. Used by permission.

GREAT AND MIGHTY ARMY 66
By Randy and Dana Rothwell

So let's shout
Let's shout the victory!
The enemy is under our feet.
So let's shout
Let's shout the victory!
For great is our King,
Great is our King,
Great is the King of kings.

©1983 Integrity's Hosanna Music, P.O. Box 16801, Mobile, AL 36616. Used by permission.

67   I WILL REJOICE
By Jill LeBlanc

I will rejoice, and be glad,
In the God of my salvation.
I will rejoice, and be glad,
All the days, all the days of my life.

For You, O Lord have made me glad,
By all that You have done.
You've given me the victory,
My battles all are won.

©1987 Integrity's Hosanna Music, P.O. Box 16801, Mobile, AL 36616. Used by permission.

68   HE IS EXALTED
By Twila Paris

He is exalted
The King is exalted on high,
I will praise Him
He is exalted forever exalted
And I will praise His name.

He is the Lord,
Forever His truth shall reign.
Heaven and earth,
Rejoice in His holy name.
He is exalted
The King is exalted on high.

©1985 Straight Way Music, Gaither Copyright Management, P.O. Box 737, Alexandria, IN 46001. Used by permission.

FOREVER GRATEFUL

By Mark Altrogge

You did not wait for me
To draw near to You,
But You clothed Yourself
With frail humanity.
You did not wait for me
To cry out to You,
But You let me
Hear Your voice calling me.

REFRAIN

And I'm forever grateful
To You.
I'm forever grateful
For the cross
I'm forever grateful to You,
That You came
To seek and save the lost.

(Repeat Verse and Refrain)

©1985 People of Destiny Music, 7881B Beechcraft Avenue, Gaithersburg, MD 20879. Used by permission.

70
SALVATION BELONGS TO OUR GOD
By Adrian Howard and Pat Turner

Salvation belongs to our God
Who sits upon the throne,
And unto the Lamb
Praise and glory,
Wisdom and thanks,
Honor and power
And strength.

REFRAIN

Be to our God
Forever and ever,
Be to our God
Forever and ever,
Be to our God forever
And ever amen.
(Repeat)

And we the redeemed
Shall be strong
In purpose and unity,
Declaring aloud
Praise and glory,
Wisdom and thanks,
Honor and power
And strength

REFRAIN

Praise and glory
Wisdom and thanks,
Honor and power,
And strength.

REFRAIN (Sing Twice)

©1985 Restoration Music Ltd., Harvestime House, 136 Hall Lane, Bradford, West Yorkshire, England BD4 7DG. Used by permission.

GOD ALONE 71
By John Keating

God alone! God alone!
In your courts, O Lord is my home.

You are my treasure, my portion, delight of my soul!
My life, my salvation, my fortress, my God and my all!

O my soul, claim nothing as your own.
For you, there is God, and God alone.

©1988 The Word of God, P.O. Box 8617, Ann Arbor, MI 48107.
Used by permission.

MY GOD AND MY ALL 72
By Jim Cowan

My God and my all
My Lord and my Savior
My King my Creator
My Father my all.

My God and my all
My Lord and my Savior
My King my Creator
My Father my all.

©1985 Jim Cowan, Steubenville Liturgical Resources, 745 Brady Avenue, Steubenville, OH 43952. Used by permission.

73 HAVE MERCY ON ME
By Gerrit Gustafson

Have mercy on me, O God,
According to Your unfailing love.
According to Your great compassion,
Blot out my transgression.

Have mercy on me, O God,
According to Your unfailing love,
Wash away my iniquity,
Cleanse me from my sin.

REFRAIN

I will be whiter than snow,
I will be whiter than snow,
I will be whiter than snow,
I will be whiter than snow,
(Repeat Verse)

By Your blood
I am whiter than snow,
I am made whiter than snow.
By Your blood
I am whiter than snow.
I am made whiter than snow.
I am made whiter than snow.
I am made whiter than snow.

©1987 Integrity's Hosanna Music, P.O. Box 16801, Mobile, AL 36616. Used by permission.

HOLY GROUND 74
By Christopher Beatty

This is Holy ground,
We're standing on Holy ground,
For the Lord is present,
And where He is, is Holy.

This is Holy ground,
We're standing on Holy ground,
For the Lord is present,
And where He is, is Holy.

This is Holy ground,
We're standing on Holy ground,
For the Lord is present,
And where He is, is Holy.

This Holy ground,
We're standing on Holy ground,
For the Lord is present,
And where He is, is Holy.

©1979 Birdwing Music, 9255 Deering Avenue, Chatsworth, CA 91311. Used by permission.

STANDING ON HOLY GROUND 75
By Geron Davis

We are standing on Holy ground,
And I know that there are angels gathering round.
Let us praise, Jesus now;
We are standing in His presence on Holy ground.

We are standing on Holy ground.
And I know that there are angels gathering round.
Let us praise, Jesus now;
We are standing in Your presence,
We are standing in Your presence,
We are standing in Your presence, on Holy ground.

©1983 Meadowgreen Music Company, Tree Publication Company, 8 Music Square West, Nashville, TN 37203. Used by permission.

76   RAISE UP AN ARMY

Words and Music By Steve and Vikki Cook

REFRAIN

Raise up an army, O God,
Awake Your people
Throughout the earth
Raise up an army, O God,
To proclaim Your Kingdom,
To declare Your Word,
To reveal Your Glory, O God.
(Repeat)

Our hope, our heart
Our vision,
To see in every land,
Your chosen people
Coming forth,
Fulfilling Your holy mission,
United as we stand,
Pledging our lives
Unto You, Lord.

REFRAIN

O God, our glorious Maker,
We marvel at Your grace,
That You would use us
in Your plan.
Rejoicing at Your favor,
Delighting in Your ways,
We'll gladly follow
Your command.

REFRAIN

Raise up an army, O God.
Awake Your people
Throughout the earth.
Raise up an army, O God,
To proclaim Your Kingdom,
To declare Your Word,
To proclaim Your Kingdom,
To declare Your Word,
To proclaim Your Kingdom,
To declare Your Word,
Raise up an army,
Raise up an army, O God.

Raise up an army, O God.
Raise up an army, O God.
Raise up an army, O God.
To proclaim Your Kingdom,
To declare Your Word,
Raise up an army, O God.

©1987 People of Destiny Music, 781B Beechcraft Avenue, Gaithersburg, MD 20879. Used by permission.

77 O COME LET US SING FOR JOY

Psalm 95: 1-3
Robert E. Mason

O come let us sing
For joy to the Lord;
Shout joyfully unto our Rock.
Let us come before Him
With thanksgiving;
Shout joyfully to Him with song.

REFRAIN

For the Lord is a great God
And a great King above
All the earth.

For the Lord is a great God
And a great King above
All the earth.

(Repeat Verse and Refrain)

For the Lord is a great God
And a great King above all the earth.
For the Lord is a great God
And a great King above all the earth.
He's the great King above all the earth.
He's the great King above all the earth.

©1987 Integrity's Hosanna Music, P.O. Box 16801, Mobile, AL 36616. Used by permission.

THE MIGHTY ONE OF ISRAEL 78

Based on Isaiah 30-29, 20, 35: 1-6
By Jime and Ginger Bendricks

The Lord shall cause His
Glorious voice to be heard,
And you shall have
A song in the night.
Come to the mountain
Of the Lord,
See His glory and
His might.
(Repeat)

REFRAIN

He's the Mighty One
Of Israel.
The Mighty One of Israel.
His voice shall be heard,
In the power of His Word,
The Mighty One of Israel.
(Repeat)

The eyes of the blind shall
Be opened and they'll see.
The ears of the
Deaf shall hear.
The lame man shall jump,
And shall leap as a hart,
The tongue of
The dumb shall sing.

REFRAIN

The Lord shall cause
His glorious beauty
To be seen.
The desert shall bloom
And rejoice.
Say to them that are
Fearful of heart,
Be strong and listen
To His voice.

REFRAIN (Twice)

©1984 Rolling Hills Music, Rt. 2, Box 494, Portland, TN 37148.
Used by permission.

79 THE GOD OF ISRAEL IS MIGHTY
By Robert E. Mason

The God of Israel is mighty,
The God of Israel knows no defeat,
He leads His people into battle,
Before Him His enemies must flee.

REFRAIN

Cry out with a shout of victory,
Lift your voice all the earth.
Sing and dance at the triumph of our King,
For He has won the war,
And spoiled the enemy.

The God of Israel is our champion,
His right arm has won the victory.
Our praises rise as incense before Him,
He fights for us and routs the enemy.

REFRAIN

©1987 Integrity's Hosanna Music, P.O. Box 16801, Mobile, AL 36616. Used by permission.

ELOHIM, ADONAI

By John Flaherty

There comes a shout of joy
From the tents of the just,
The name of Elohim, Adonai,
There comes a shout of joy
From the tents of the just,
The name of Elohim, Adonai.

REFRAIN

Elohim! Adonai,
The name of God most High!
Elohim! Adonai,
The name of God most High!

There comes a cry for help
From the voice of the poor,
The name of Elohim, Adonai.
There comes a cry for help
From the voice of the poor,
The name of Elohim, Adonai.

REFRAIN

There comes a song of praise
From the lips of Israel,
The name of Elohim, Adonai.
There comes a song of praise
From the lips of Israel,
The name of Elohim, Adonai.

REFRAIN

©1989 Steubenville Liturgical Resources, 745 Brady Avenue, Steubenville, OH 43952. Used by permission.

81 ALL CONSUMING FIRE

Hebrews 12:29
By Randy N. Wright

All consuming fire,
You're my heart's desire,
And I love You
Dearly, dearly, Lord.

REFRAIN

You're my meditation,
And my consolation,
And I love You
Dearly, dearly, Lord.

Glory to the Lamb,
I exalt the great I AM.
Reigning on Your glorious throne,
You are my eternal home.

ⓒ1987 Integrity's Hosanna Music, P.O. Box 16801, Mobile, AL 36616. Used by permission.

82 TO HIM WHO SITS ON THE THRONE

By Debbye Graafsma

To Him who sits on the throne,
And unto the Lamb,
To Him who sits on the throne,
And unto the Lamb,
Be blessing and glory
And Honor and power forever!
Be blessing and glory
And Honor and power forever!

ⓒ1984 Integrity's Hosanna Music, P.O. Box 16801, Mobile, AL 36616. Used by permission.

WE ARE AN OFFERING

By Dwight Liles

We lift our voices,
We lift our hands,
We lift our lives up to You
We are an offering.
Lord use our voices,
Lord use our hands,
Lord use our lives,
They are Yours,
We are an offering,

REFRAIN

All that we have,
All that we are,
All that we hope to be,
We give to You,
We give to You.

We lift our voices,
We lift our hands,
We lift our lives up to You
We are an offering.
We are an offering.

Repeat Refrain and Verse (last line twice)

©1984 Bug and Bear Music, LCS Music Group, Inc., P.O. Box 7409, Dallas, TX 75209. Used by permission.

84 WITH ALL MY HEART
By Jim Cowan

Thou shalt love the Lord your God
With all your heart, and all your soul
With all your mind, and all your strength
So shall you love the Lord your God.
(Repeat)

We have been chosen
From all nations,
To approach the throne of God.
We have been ransomed
Through adoption,
In a covenant with blood.
We are called to follow Jesus.
As companions of the cross
To give ourselves completely
And count all else as loss.

I shall love You Lord my God
With all my heart, and all my soul
With all my mind, and all my strength
So shall I love You Lord my God.
(Repeat)

©1989 Jim Cowan, Steubenville Liturgical Resources, 745 Brady Avenue, Steubenville, OH 43952. Used by permission.

SING UNTO THE LORD   85
By Leon Patillo

Sing unto the Lord a new song,
Let His praises fill the temple.
He is the King of Kings
And the Lord of Lords,
Bow down before Him.
(Repeat)

REFRAIN

Hallelujah, Glory to God.
Hallelujah, Glory to God.

Sing unto the Lord a new song,
For He loves to hear our praises.
Let all of creation sing
Glory to our God
Bow down before Him.

REFRAIN

©1984 Word Music, Winona Lake, IN 46590. Used by permission.

86 SURROUND US LORD
Bobby Price

As the mountains surround Jerusalem
So the Lord surrounds His people.
As the mountains surround Jerusalem
So the Lord surrounds His people.

CHORUS
Surround us Lord
Surround us Lord
We need to be in Your presence
Surround us Lord.

Copyright © 1990 Bobby Price. Dawn Treader Music, Adm. Gaither Copyright Management, P.O. Box 737, Alexandria, Indiana 46001. Used with permission.

87 ALL CREATION WORSHIPS YOU
Kirk Dearman and Jim Mills

You are God,
And we praise You.
You are Lord,
We acclaim You.
You are eternal Father
All creation worships You,
All creation worships You,
All creation worships You,
A-men.

Copyright © 1988 Kirk Dearman and Jim Mills. Integrity's Hosanna Music, P.O. Box 16813, Mobile, Alabama 36616. Used with permission.

FOREVER TO REIGN   88
Jim Cowan

Worthy, worthy,
Worthy the Lamb who was slain.
Worthy, worthy,
Worthy the Lamb who was slain.

To receive dominion
All honor and thanks
To receive all worship and praise
To receive the Kingdom
Forever to reign.

Worthy the Lamb who was slain.
Worthy the Lamb
Worthy the Lamb
Worthy the Lamb who was slain.

Copyright © 1991 Jim Cowan. Franciscan University, Steubenville, Ohio 43952. Used with permission.

CROWN HIM LORD OF LORDS   89
Jim Cowan

All glory and praise to the Lamb.
All glory and praise to the Lamb.
For He that was slain
Is risen again
All glory and praise to the Lamb.
(Repeat first time only)

CHORUS
    Praise Him,
    Praise Him,
    Magnify His Name and
    Praise Him,
    Praise Him,
    Glorify His Name and
    Crown Him Lord of Lords, (Repeat)
    Amen.

Copyright © 1985 S.L.R. ©1991 Jim Cowan (New Arrangement). Franciscan University, Steubenville, Ohio 43952. Used with permission.

I WANT TO KNOW YOU

Brian Doerksen and Cindy Reithmeier

I want to know You
Lord I must know You
I want to be found in You
I want to be clothed in Your truth.

So I fix my eyes on You
Lord I must see You
I put my faith in You
I spend my life on You.

CHORUS
   I want to know You
   I want to love You
   I want to know You more.
   Jesus, Jesus.
   Jesus, Jesus.

Copyright © Brian Doerksen and Cindy Reithmeier. Mercy Publishing, P.O. Box 65004, Anaheim, California 92815. Used with permission.

FAITHFUL TO YOUR CALL
Jim Cowan

One thing I ask for
That shall I seek
To dwell in the house of the Lord
And there to behold
The face of my Lord
And bow down in worship before Him.

CHORUS
    Worthy, worthy
    Worthy, You are worthy
    Worthy, worthy
    Lord of all (to verse)
    Worthy, worthy
    Lord of all.

There is no treasure
Here on this earth
That equals one day with You, Lord
And here in Your presence
I know perfect joy
I lift up my voice to adore You. (CHORUS)

Lord, I want to be Your servant
More than anything at all
Just to know that I've been faithful
To Your call
Just to love You
Lord I love You. (CHORUS)

Copyright © 1990 Jim Cowan. Franciscan University, Steubenville, Ohio 43952. Used with permission.

92   I BOW MY KNEE
Bonnie Deuschle

I bow my knee before Your throne
I know my life is not my own
I offer up a song of praise
To bring You pleasure Lord.

CHORUS
  Hallelujah
  Hallelujah
  Hallelujah
  Glory to the King.
  Hallelujah
  Hallelujah
  Hallelujah.
  Glory to the King.
  Hallelujah, glory to the King.

I seek the Giver not the gift
My heart's desire is to lift You
High above all earthly kings
To bring You pleasure Lord. (Chorus)

Copyright © 1990 Bonnie Deuschle. Integrity's Hosanna Music, P.O. Box 16813, Mobile, Alabama 36616. Used with permission.

A SHIELD ABOUT ME

Don Thomas and Charles Williams

Thou, oh Lord
Art a shield about me
You're my glory
And the lifter of my head.

Thou, oh Lord
Art a shield about me
You're my glory
And the lifter of my head.

Hallelujah, hallelujah,
Hallelujah,
You're the lifter of my head.
Hallelujah, hallelujah,
Hallelujah,
You're the lifter of my head.

Copyright © 1980 Don Thomas and Charles Williams. Spoon Music, (Adm. by Word Music), 5221 O'Connor Boulevard, Ste. 1000, Irving, Texas 75039. Used with permission.

REFINER'S FIRE
Brian Doerksen

Purify my heart
Let me be as gold and precious silver
Purify my heart
Let me be as gold, pure gold.

CHORUS
   Refiner's fire
   My heart's one desire
   Is to be holy
   Set apart for You, Lord
   I want to be holy
   Set apart for You, my Master
   Ready to do Your will.

Purify my heart
Cleanse me from within and make me holy
Purify my heart
Cleanse me from my sin, deep within.

Copyright © 1990 Brian Doerksen. Mercy Publishing, P.O. Box 65004, Anaheim, California 92815. Used with permission.

COME INTO MY HEART

Jim Cowan

Come into my heart
Come into my heart
Come into my heart, Lord
Come into my heart.

Come into my life...

Cleanse me of my sin...

I give my life to life...

Take all that I am...

I will follow You...

Holy Spirit come...

Come into my heart...

Copyright © 1990 Jim Cowan. Franciscan University, Steubenville, Ohio 43952. Used with permission.

96 I WILL PLEDGE THIS SONG TO YOU
Jim Cowan

CHORUS
    You are holy, You are holy
    And my life is in Your hands
    You are worthy, You are worthy,
    Take my life and all I am.

Every dream I've known
Every heartache too
They have all been shared with You
All the times I've failed
Been untrue to You.
I have known Your mercy too. (CHORUS)

Now the way shines clear
And Your presence here
Gives me strength to carry through.
Lord You are my way
And so every day
I will pledge this song to You. (CHORUS)

Copyright © 1991 Jim Cowan. Franciscan University, Steubenville, Ohio 43952. Used with permission.

WE EXALT YOU

Kirk Dearman and Jim Mills

CHORUS
    We exalt You
    We exalt You
    We exalt You
    Exalted King on high. (Repeat)

We are called of You
Gathered from all nations
Called as priests to You
To demonstrate Your praise. (CHORUS)

We are living stones
Formed by Your own righteousness
Joined in unity
To celebrate Your love. (CHORUS)

Copyright © 1990 Kirk Dearman and Jim Mills. Integrity's Hosanna Music, P.O. Box 16813, Mobile, Alabama 36616. Used with permission.

98   IN THIS UPPER ROOM
Jim Cowan

Lord we come to You,
In this upper room,
To wait, and watch, and pray.
For we are Your Church,
And we need rebirth,
Send forth Your Spirit in our day.

REFRAIN

    Lord, send forth Your Spirit,
    And renew the face of the earth.
    Lord, send forth Your Spirit,
    And renew the face of the earth.
    Renew the face of the earth.

Repeat Verse and REFRAIN

Lord, send forth Your Spirit.
Lord, send forth Your Spirit.
Lord, send forth Your Spirit.
And we shall be renewed,
And we shall be renewed.

Holy Spirit come,
Holy Spirit come,
Holy Spirit come,
Holy Spirit come.

Copyright © 1992 Jim Cowan, Franciscan University, Steubenville, OH 43952.

SPIRIT OF GOD MEDLEY

Jim Cowan

A. FIRE OF GOD

Spirit of God, Spirit of Holiness,
Spirit of Love,
Fall afresh on me,
Fall afresh on me,
Fall afresh on me,
Fall afresh on me,
Fall afresh on me.

Fire of God, Fire of Holiness,
Fire of Love,
Fall afresh on me,
Fall afresh on me,
Fall afresh on me,
Fall afresh on me,
Fall afresh on me.

B. WHEN THE SPIRIT SETS US FREE

When the Spirit sets us free,
We are free indeed.
Don't submit again to the law of slavery.
When the Spirit sets us free.
We are free indeed.
Don't submit again to the law of slavery.

C. NOT BY MIGHT

And it's not by might, not by power,
But by My Spirit says the Lord.
And it's not by might, not by power,
But by My Spirit says the Lord.

Repeat Verse 2 FIRE OF GOD
Repeat NOT BY MIGHT
Repeat WHEN THE SPIRIT SETS US FREE

D. JESUS REIGNS

Jesus reigns and blessed be my Rock
And exalted be His name forevermore.
Jesus reigns and blessed be my Rock
And exalted be His name forevermore.
And exalted be His name forevermore.

Copyright © 1992 Jim Cowan. Franciscan University, Steubenville, Ohio 43952.

100 LET US REJOICE AND BE GLAD
Jim Cowan

REFRAIN:

This is the day that the Lord has made
Let us rejoice and be glad.
This is the day that the Lord has made
Let us rejoice, let us rejoice,
Let us rejoice and be glad.

Open the gates of righteousness
And let us give thanks to the Lord.
Christ is the gate through which we enter,
The Way through Heaven's door.
The stone which the builders rejected,
Has become the cornerstone.
What couldn't be done by our striving,
Has been done by God alone.

REFRAIN

The Lord is my strength and my salvation,
His love and His grace I proclaim.
I shall not die, but live to priase Him,
Proclaiming how great is His name.
Thy right hand is exalted,
You have triumphed o'er the foe.
You are my God I exalt You,
I will praise You more and more.
Let those who fear the Lord,
Say His love is everlasting.
Let those who love the Lord,
Say His love is unending.

REFRAIN

Copyright © 1992 Jim Cowan, Franciscan University, Steubenville, OH 43952.

I LONG TO SEE YOUR FACE 101
Jim Cowan

Lord I long to see Your face
As we gather in this place,
Just to worship with the angels 'round Your throne.
For You are the Lord I love,
My Father and my God,
And my heart cries out to know Your living word.

REFRAIN I
    For without You I have nothing,
    Please don't turn Your face away
    Let Your Spirit rest upon me as I pray.
    As I lift my heart to Heaven
    Let my prayer rise up to You.
    I worship You, I worship You,
    I worship You my God.

Lord we long to see Your face,
As we gather in this place,
Just to worship with the angels 'round Your throne.
For You are the Lord we love,
Our Father and our God,
And our hearts cry out to know Your living word.

REFRAIN II
    For without You we have nothing,
    Please don't turn Your face away.
    Let Your Spirit rest upon us as we pray.
    As we lift our hearts to Heaven,
    Let our prayers rise up to You
    We worship You, we worship You,
    We worship You our God.

REFRAIN III
    For without You we have nothing,
    Please don't turn Your face away.
    Let Your spirit rest upon us as we pray.
    As we lift our hearts to Heaven,
    Let our prayers rise up to You
    We worship You, we worship You,
    We worship You our God.
    I long for You, I thirst for You,
    I worship You my God.

Copyright © 1992 Jim Cowan, Franciscan University, Steubenville, OH 43952.

102   IN YOUR LIGHT
Jim Cowan

REFRAIN:
    Your love O Lord reaches to the heavens,
    Your faithfulness is higher than the skies.
    Your righteousness is like majestic mountains,
    Your mercy Lord, like the depths of the sea.

Your hand O Lord sustains all Your creation.
How priceless is Your unfailing love.
Both great and small find a home among Your people.
A refuge sure in the shelter of Your wings.

REFRAIN

We feast upon the abundance of Your household,
You give us drink from the rivers of great joy.
In You O Lord is the fountain of life
And in Your light do we find life forevermore.

    Your love O Lord reaches to the heavens,
    Your faithfulness is higher than the skies.
    In You O Lord is the fountain of life
    And in Your light do we find life forevermore.

Copyright © 1992 Jim Cowan. Franciscan University, Steubenville, Ohio 43952.

103   I DEDICATE MY HEART
Jim Cowan

Lord I dedicate my heart,
To be Your dwelling place.
A holy temple set apart,
A sacrifice of praise.
All the idols of the past,
Must now be cast away.
Lord I dedicate my heart,
To be Your dwelling place.

REFRAIN:
    Holy, Holy, Lord, Holy, Holy, Lord
    Holy, Holy, Lord, Holy, Holy, Lord
    Holy, Holy, Lord, Holy, Holy, Lord
    Holy, Holy, Lord, Holy, Holy, Lord

Copyright © 1992 Jim Cowan, Franciscan University, Steubenville, OH 43952.

SHINE, JESUS, SHINE

Graham Kendrick

REFRAIN
Shine, Jesus, shine.
Fill this land
With the Father's glory.
Blaze, Spirit, blaze.
Set our hearts on fire.
Flow, river, flow.
Flood the nations
With grace and mercy.
Send forth Your Word Lord
And let there be light.

Lord, the light of
Your love is shining.
In the midst of
The darkness shining.
Jesus, Light of the world
Shine upon us.
Set us free by the truth
You now bring us.
Shine on me,
Shine on me.

Repeat REFRAIN

Lord, I come to
Your awesome presence,
From the shadows
Into Your radiance.
By the blood
I may enter Your brightness.
Search me, try me
Consume all my darkness.
Shine on me,
Shine on me.

Repeat REFRAIN
Shine, Jesus, shine
Shine, Jesus, shine.

As we gaze on
Your kingly brightness,
So our faces display
Your likeness,
Ever changing from
Glory to glory.
Mirrored here may our lives
Tell Your story.
Shine on me,
Shine on me.

Repeat REFRAIN Twice
    Shine, Jesus, shine (Echo)
    Shine, Jesus, shine (Echo)
    And let there be light

Copyright © 1987 Make Way Music, Adm. in U.S. & Canada by Integrity's Hosanna! Music.

105   DRAW ME NEARER MEDLEY
Jim Cowan

A. MORE OF YOU

Draw me nearer Lord,
I want more and more of You.
Draw me nearer Jesus,
I want more and more of You.

REFRAIN
    More of You,
    I want more of You.
    More of You, Lord,
    And less of me.

Teach me how to love,
'Till I'm more and more like You
Teach me how to love Lord,
'Till I'm more and more like You.

REFRAIN

B. THAT FIRST LOVE

Restore to me that first love,
That I had when I gave my life to You.
Restore to me that first love
That I had when I gave my life to You.

Create in me a clean heart,
And renew a right spirit within me.
Create in me a clean heart,
And renew a right spirit within me.

C. REFRAIN (INTO YOUR HANDS)
   All of my dreams, All of my days.
   All of my life,
   I place into Your hands

I place my life into Your hands.
I place my life into Your hands.
All of my dreams, all of my days,
I place my life into Your hands. (Repeat)

REFRAIN (INTO YOUR HANDS)

D. IMMERSE ME

Immerse me in Your mercy.
Wash me white as snow.
Immerse me in Your mercy.
Wash me 'till I'm whole. (Repeat)

E. REFRAIN — IN YOUR NAME
   Jesus, Jesus,
   Your name sets all the captives free
   Jesus, Jesus,
   Your name means everything to me.

We gather in Your name,
With our hearts in one accord,
Singing holy, holy Lord.
We gather to proclaim,
The greatness of that name,
That washes all our guilt and shame away.
That washes all our guilt and shame away.

REFRAIN

F. I LOVE YOU LORD MY KING

I love You Lord my strength,
I love You Lord my King.
More than anything,
I love You Lord my strength,
I love You Lord my King.

I love You more than riches
I love you more than fame
More than anything
I love you Lord my strength
I love you Lord my King.

G. REFRAIN — YOU ARE MY HOPE O GOD
    O God, my God,
    My life is in Your hands.
    O God, my God,
    I give You all I am.

You are my hope O God,
I will place my trust in You.
You are my hope O God,
I will place my trust in You.

You are my strength, O God,
In my weakness I am strong.
You are my strength, O God,
In my weakness I am strong.

REFRAIN

H. GOD OF MY LIFE, I BELIEVE

All that I have, all that I seek,
All All that I hope for, I lay down at Your feet.
All that I am, all that I need
All that I long for, I find when I believe, in You.

REFRAIN
    You are my Rock,
    I build my life on You.
    You are my God and my King.
    You are my strength,
    I place my trust in You.
    God of my life I believe.

Copyright © 1992 Jim Cowan. Franciscan University, Steubenville, Ohio 43952.